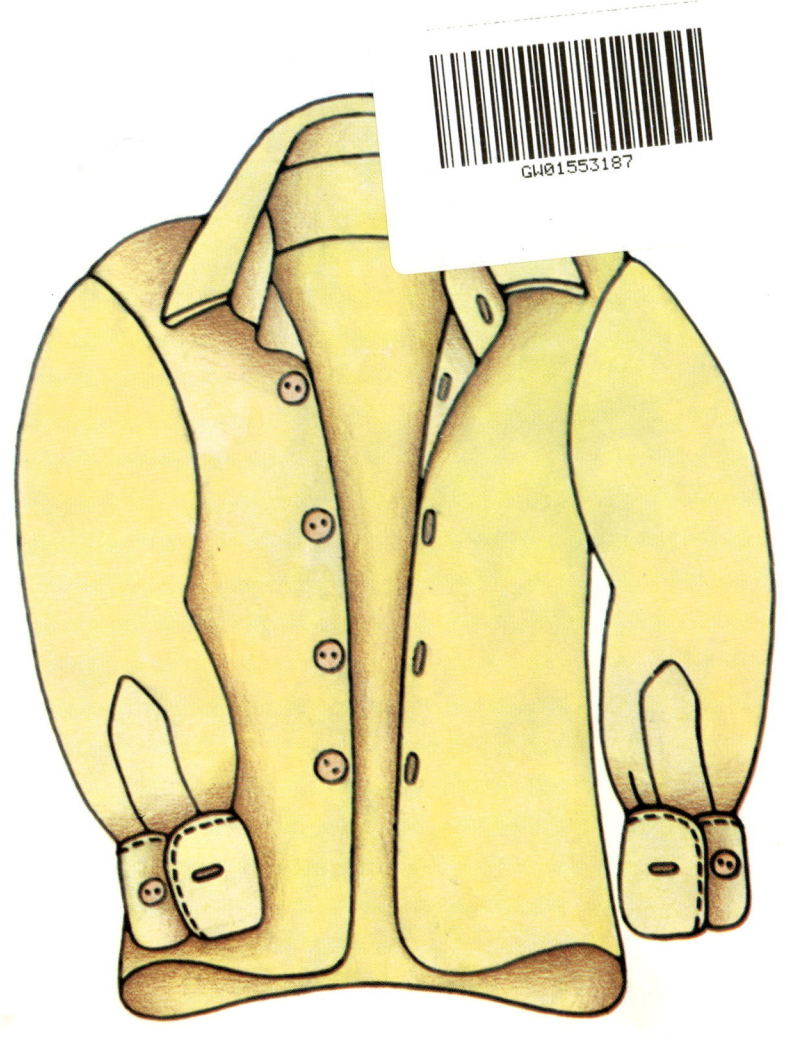

How do you do this up?

Button it up.

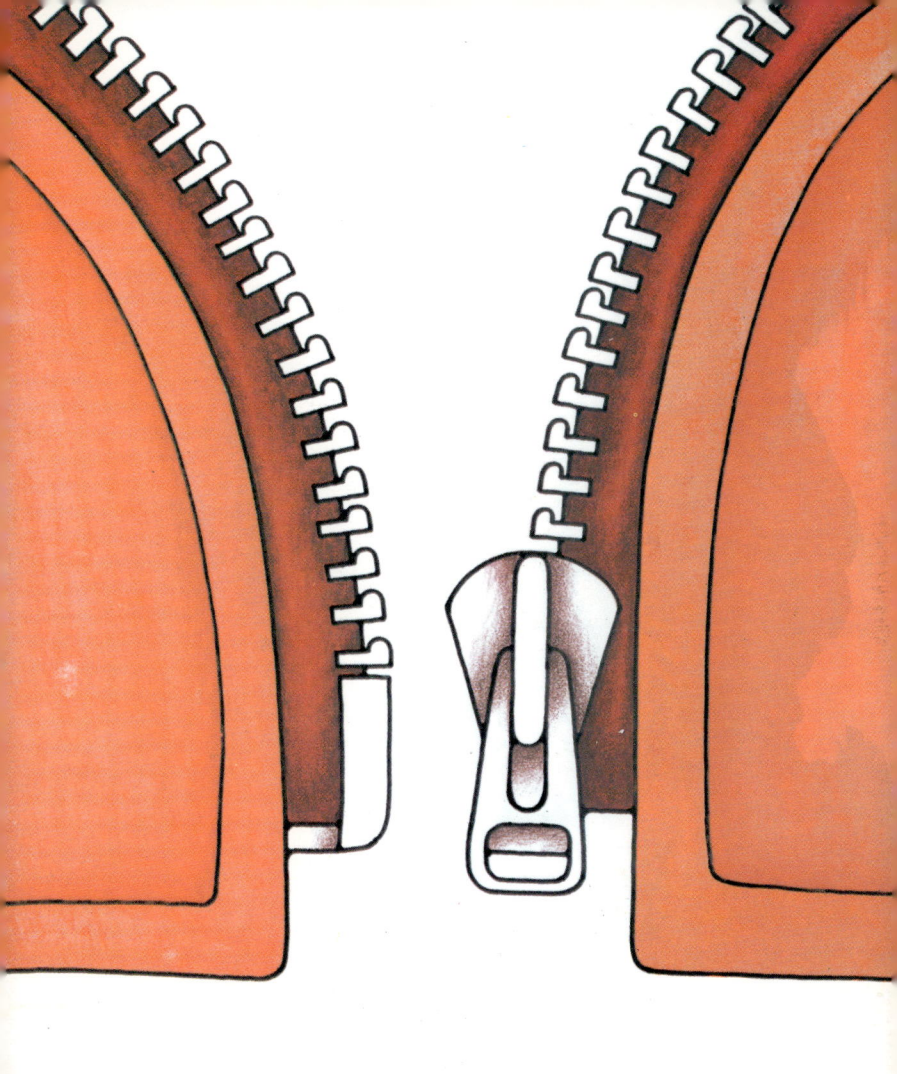

How do you do this up?

Zip up the zip.

How do you do this up?

Tie it in a bow.

How do you do this up?

Tie it in a knot

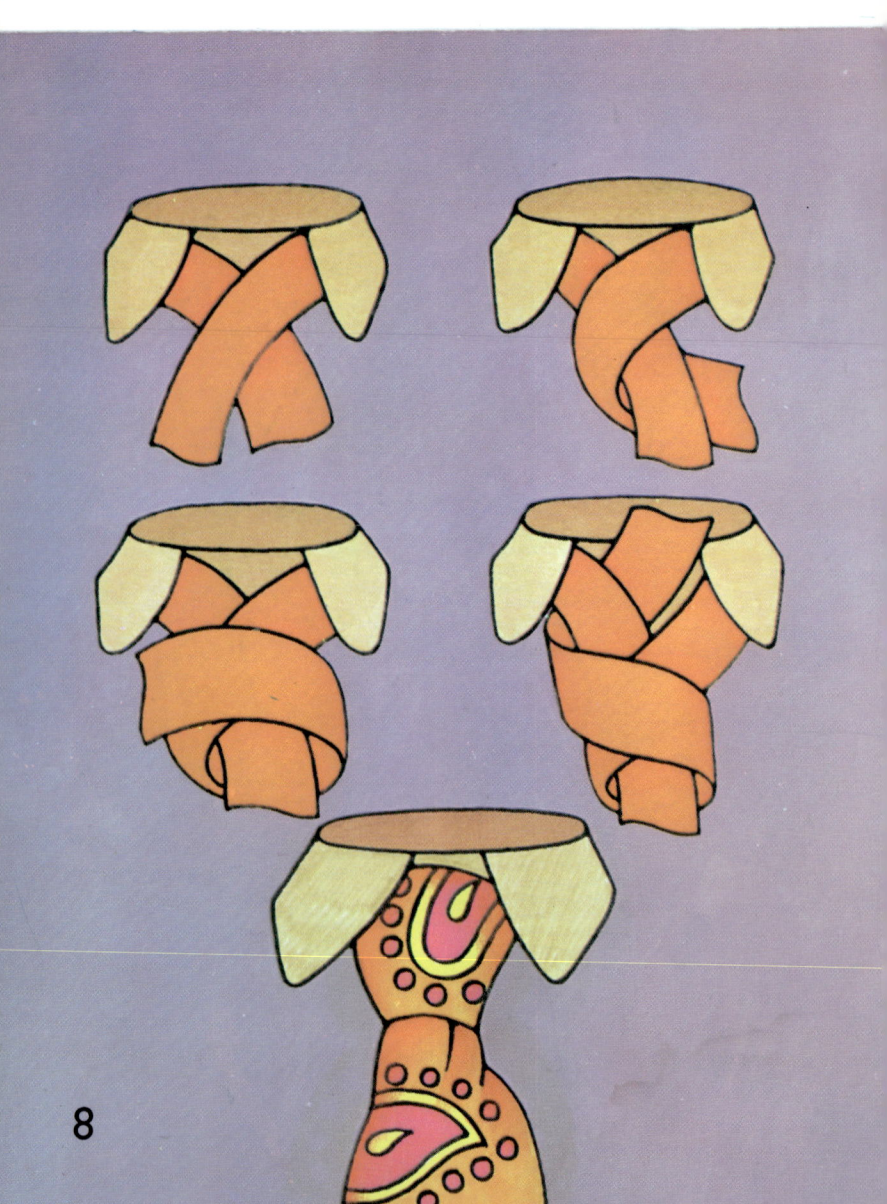

How do you do this up?

Tie up the lace.

How do you do this up?

Do up the toggles.

How do you do this up?

Do up the buckle.

How do you do this up?

Press the press studs.

Do your ears hang low?
Can you swing them
to and fro?
Can you tie them in a knot?
Can you tie them in a bow?